The Unraveling Script

Poems

by Maggie Kennedy

Pine Row Press

for my mother
for kindling my imagination

The Unraveling Script

© 2023 by Maggie Kennedy

Published by Pine Row Press

Ft. Mitchell, KY 41011

ISBN: 978-1-963110-00-5

December 2023

First Edition

10 9 8 7 6 5 4 3 2 1

==========

Publisher's website at pinerow.com

Contents

I

Religion Arrives in the Subdivision	13
The Unraveling Script	15
September Clouds	18
The Murders	19
The Night Watchman	22
Crazy	24
City Zoo	26
Hysteranthous	29
A Sculptor to the Sculpted	31
Block Party Between COVID Waves	34
Stumbling After	36
Lot	38
Raven	39

II

Sonogram	43
Home	45
John Appleseed Speaks His Mind	47
Uprising	49
Maud Gonne's Tabby	53
Exponential Decay	54
Insomnia	56

A Suburban Winter	58
Boogie Board	60
Search Engine Optimization	61
Blood Draw	64
The Sisters Part Ways	66
Simple	68
Parenting Styles	70
Writing for the Man	71

III

Kisses	75
Spotting Hobos	78
The Other Side	80
How to Die Like a Collapsing Star	83
My Big Idea	84
Cardinal	86
Bumper Crop	88
Tarzan Goes to His Resting Grounds	91
Child's Body Found in Park Lagoon, Chicago	92
Unfettered	93
Shadows	94
You and I	96
Looking Up from the News	99

Acknowledgments	101
About the Poet	103

I

Religion Arrives in the Subdivision

Two young men gripping Bibles stick out
like the few and far between trees.

They come every summer. Different ones.
Same white button-downs, crewcuts, ties.
Begin ringing bells on Pleasant Lane,
move down Magnolia Drive before
turning down our street.

My brother and I are dropping stones
down the sewer, counting thousands
till they splash.

The sun hits oil spots,
turning the street into water
so the men seem to walk on waves.

Our block stiffens: the rush of hoses,
whir of Big Wheels, thump of basketballs
quiets. A jet rumbles overhead
and the neighbor's hound sets off
a chorus of howls.

My mother waves us inside,
pulls drapes, mutes the TV.
We pretend we're not home,
listening for footsteps on our stairs,
muffled voices, and a second
ring of the doorbell.

When they head to the next house,
my mother crosses herself,
says a Hail Mary for the born again,
and one for us
who hide from them.

The Unraveling Script

If I could take it back, Miss Halstead, I would,
that moment decades ago after you called me
to the front of the class to commend
my penmanship, repeating your go-to proclamation:
"Cursive is a continuous line ..."

Riley McGuirk crossed his eyes, meaning I was with
or against them so I stuck out my behind,
mocking you, Miss Halstead,
and a wave of giggles rumbled over desks.

The hurt in your eyes was a surprise.
I had caused your powdered countenance to crack,
and the difficulty of your life rushed over me,
us children sticking our tongues at your back
as you pushed your squeaking walker down the halls.
That was punishment enough.

But I appreciated the detention where I copied
sentences in cursive, trying to make it up
to you, Miss Halstead, looping back, looping forward,
pausing at the end of sentences to dot
my *i*'s, cross my *t*'s, while the other kids

broke out along tree-lined blocks that fanned
from school. They would be climbing, sliding down
plowed snow hills, stomping iced-over puddles
for the scintillating crack, and Riley would be stealing
another girl's hat to toss high.

That was winter '73 after 12 days of Christmas
bombings crumbled Hanoi and our troops trickled

in from Vietnam. It left Suzie's dad without a leg,
Stan's sister an addict. It brought squalls to
unearth mulching leaves rising to our classroom.

I was learning. The indecipherable script.
My own, the world's, and you had something to teach me,
Miss Halstead. Everything about you a past era,
your up-do and A-line dresses. Even the polio that
infected you something we'd been vaccinated against.

In detention radiators cranked, and you and I
took turns turning paper. I was safe in my secret.
I loved how cursive adorned the mundane,
made lovely our sentences, how I seemed to lift
and widen as my hand looped and curled.

Yet when you presented me with the fountain pen,
in front of the class, "given to devoted students
of the craft," I melted under the snickering.
What could a 4th grader know of devotion?

I knew only that cursive was old-fashioned,
pretty but unnecessary like china patterns and
silk slips. That was before my family packed our home
on York Road, and I became the new kid teased.

It was before Nixon assured us he was
not a crook. Before we watched his helicopter
leaving the White House lawn
then helicopters leaving Saigon behind.

I would soon learn to type and appreciate
the efficiency of getting to the end of a page
in 50 words a minute. It felt more like a gain.

I didn't notice the unraveling.

Miss Halstead, do you recall the sparrows?
A string of them swooped onto the windowsill
that day and started trilling. You cracked a rare smile,
and we both hovered in the song.

That was when I realized that beauty,
extraneous as a sparrow, feels like forgiveness.

I think of this today when I can't read the to-do list
I just wrote. My handwriting has become illegible.
It's winter again, and the clouds feel fixed. Other wars
are being fought, more lies than anyone can count,
and I snap at my husband for asking what's wrong.

It won't change anything. But I pick up my pen
to try again, looping forward, looping back,
and the lovely lettering pulls me along like a rope.

Speak to me, Miss Halstead, of devotion.
Remind me to dot my "*i*'s," cross my "*t*'s."
Tell me again it's all a continuous line.

September Clouds

Some clouds could
never understand:
floating puffs of moisture,
decorations with no entanglements,
or striated streaks stretched
too thin to take on
another trouble.

Others speak,
sum up a season:
rifts ablaze, valleys solemn,
having absorbed in their
slow migration

salty sweat
stagnant breath
morning dew
morning pee
cry a river
laugh till it hurts
spit in the ocean
spit in the eye
spilled milk
spilled words.

Standing beneath
is to be enfolded,
known, accepted,
part of the unnerving blue.

The Murders

Everyone confirms, yes, the Clydesdales
marched through town that Fourth.
Huge barrel-chested horses in white-stocking feet
pulling flag-bedecked carriages crammed
with bureaucrats tossing candy
to any child who dared to dive.

But no one verifies the murders.
My father clouded in barbecue smoke,
aunts and uncles round the picnic table,
us kids in the willow's curtains
killing time till dusk when
fireworks would crack open color:
spatter, spatter, bang, spatter, spatter.

I remember my mother hurrying
from the house. "On the radio," she said.
"The Clydesdales, dead.
Someone shot them dead."

**

I was still small enough to squeeze through
for a front-row view as the parade rounded
the corner, led by eight bay-colored Scots,
well-muscled peasants bred to haul and plow,
cultivated for their prettiness,
the Sabino gene that whitens their noses,
feathers their formidable calves.

I felt certain they'd walked straight out
of a fairy tale or, more precisely, the commercial,

bells tingling as they clipped along,
pulling a load of Budweiser to tall gates
that crack open a lush estate before
returning to regular programming.

Here they were, these magnificent beasts,
damp with sweat, grunting from their efforts,
transporting us to just before sunset,
when the light takes on a celebratory
air, and why not pull up a chair?

**

But no one else recalls the shootings.
Decades later, my sisters look confused
and mildly worried for my sanity,
and I realize we all had different childhoods
though we went through them together.

I wonder, did I make the whole thing up?
A false memory formed by a dream
or concocted as retribution,
my family stacking up palely after
the Clydesdales trotted from sight.

**

Outside our crumbling rental at the edge
of our picturesque suburb, yards from
the sorry-to-see-you leave sign, behind
the willow's drapery that hung despondent
in the curling humidity, I spied on
the grown-ups raising beers,
slapping mosquitoes from ankles

buried in dandelions, shielding their
eyes from the sun's glare.

Perhaps I was disappointed by
the predictability of their conversation,
annoyed at my sisters giggling,
engaged in games I had suddenly outgrown.

I pictured the Clydesdales grazing,
fog edging the pasture,
my white Keds dyeing green from the grass,
and I imagined lifting my water gun,
horses toppling like paper dolls,
no noise, no pain,
just a barely perceptible blip and switch.

My defense: It was them or my family.

The Night Watchman

Other children dipped brushes
in blues, reds, yellows,
painted trees, flowers,
sunshine. I mixed palettes
of black, discovered early
that adding enough black
brings you back to black.

I never needed lullabies,
pulled the shade against
moonlight, squeezed my eyes
tight, trying to see
inside black, as though
night opened a trap door,
colors as radiantly dark
as gold is bright.

Decades now, and
only glimpses.
A ray of carbon that
glittered fluorescence
and once, when the fog snuffed
the streetlights, a shiver
of onyx that seeped like dawn.

I make my living off the night,
walk dim empty corridors,
flip forgotten lights,
wishing for an evolutionary tick,
tapetum lucidum,
glowing pupils of an owl.

I turn corners quickly,
imagining long-limbed creatures
camouflaged by shadows,
knocking stars croquet-like
through the heavens.

Crazy

The teacher tells us of Van Gogh,
and Riley McGuirk and I spend
a week washing blackboards
for painting the sides of our faces
red, for running into the classroom
screaming "crazy,"
that we'd cut off our ears.

We do it for the laugh.
The teacher quakes,
our friends erupt in giggles, and
Van Gogh's bottomless oranges,
tumultuous blues dissolve among
swings creaking, lawnmowers buzzing,
the foliage-soaked light
that cuts the streetlamps glare.

7 am prompt.
Sausages spit, Dad whistles with the radio,
Mom's kiss Tic Tacs and coffee.
Last night's despair, clandestine utterings
just dream talk.

Splash, clink, pour another.
Our gentle uncle, so handsome,
fell or did he jump off the third-floor flat?
Our grandmother who refused
to get out of bed, weighed down
by what was supposed to
but never happened.

Van Gogh's prints hang for weeks.

Skies swallow, fields detonate.
Pigments climb then plunge,
heights pure oxygen, realm down
tumbling realm of radiant color
that scrapes my heart raw
like a skinned knee.

A rubber band whizzes by.
Riley crosses his eyes, and I play
along, twisting my features a crazy face.

City Zoo

after Rilke's The Panther

The sun that slept all day shows up
only to fade.
Another day caged.

The leopard is pacing, half turn repeat,
half turn repeat, the same 10-foot path
hardened to concrete from pacing
half turn repeat.

In the gawking crowd, a boy teases
his sister, "You'd make a tasty snack."
The girl ignores him,
mesmerized by the leopard,
his shoulders heaving with each step
of his formidable paws.

The girl had run with the other kids
to see the spotted cat from picture books,
but now there is a stone in her throat,
a spider tying up her heart.

The leopard's sleek head skims the ground
as he paces then turns, paces then turns,
mouth an open sneer,
pink tongue and chiseled fangs.

"Dear sweetness, dear sweetness," the child whispers.

The big cat swings his head to glare,
long enough for her to see

his glassy tea-green eyes
shift between fury and despair.

"Don't pity me, small one.
I would scratch out your freckles in one swipe."

The girl puts a hand to her cheek.
"Don't be mean. I just want to help."

"You can't. I don't know what I need.
I don't know its name. Only its absence."

The leopard returns to pacing.
This is what his father did
and his father before him
and so on back to the leopard
who stalked moonless nights
to snatch screeching, squirming prey,
who knew the taste of warm blood,
who knew how it felt for tables to turn,
to be chased into a cage,
to be caged.

This leopard is not that leopard.
This leopard knows only gaggles of eyes
following his every move,
twice-a-day meals dead on arrival
and this unnamable hunger
that causes him to pace
until something loosens and he can sleep
before rising to pace
half turn repeat.

The girl blinks to stop from crying
before her brother taunts her.
She knows only to follow her family
to the bear exhibit.
She is a visitor among throngs of visitors
among caged animals.
This is what her mother did
and her mother before her
and so on back to the girl who lived
at the edge of wilderness,
raised to log, brick, and fence,
who knew what it felt like to trap
howling, growling beasts,
to hear slammed closed a cage,
to cage.

This girl is not that girl.
This girl knows the artificial sweetness
of a rainbow snow cone,
the solace of a stuffed leopard from the gift shop
to add to the collection of animals
she kisses one by one at the end of her bed,
"Dear sweetness, dear sweetness."

Hysteranthous

Her parents are too busy following
along in their hymn books to notice
their pint-size daughter has escaped the pew.

She twirls down the aisle round
and round, leaps and pirouettes,
her tutu a glittering purple swirl,
heels of her gym shoes flickering rainbows.

Dance, little one, dance
before your mother, scurrying to retrieve you,
pulls you back.

The girl's black curls slip from her ponytail
as she passes the plodding chorus,
a skip, spin she nears the altar.

I want to join her, shimmy and sway
along the pews. Just like I wanted to climb
the flowering magnolia outside church
to finger the leathery pink petals.

But I don't. I didn't.
I am not young enough or old enough
to dare embarrassment for a chance at rapture.

Dance, little one, dance.
Outside, precocious bloomers are coming to life.
Under this roof, only hesitant souls.

The priest looks up to see the nymph curtsy.
A flash of annoyance in his eyes, or is it jealousy,

before he smiles at the mother bending
towards her child. All these years, perhaps,
he too has been waiting for grace.

Dance, little one, dance.
Never forget you flowered
before you leafed.

A Sculptor to the Sculpted
Giacometti to His Walking Man

You have to be cut down a peg,
whittled by circumstance,
a shaving here, a slice there

until the slights, jeers, fumbles,
even my duplicity,
this paring of your heart

a bargained gale, more promise
than disillusion; you must want
to go home then realize

this is your home now; I must cut
from you the girth of all you expected
was yours unconditionally until

you are pin-thin, slight enough
to settle with the other scrapes,
elbow to elbow, yet never quite touch

until you are the rhythm of the train
churning to and from the desk
where you are a bent head

among countless bent heads until I tug
your chin up to witness the chant
of geese echoing down the skyscrapers

because you must be a fabricator,
a prevaricator to draw a certain splendor
from the steam rising off the sewer ducts,

to keep walking despite your lodged feet;
I must take you to the edge of tears by
the unexpected kindness of pigeons;

you will not know then but this is what
saves you, gives you audacity, impudence
to love another stick figure for how

she sees you seeing her, and for a time,
this is all there will be,
astonishment at your luck,

how your outlines fit together as if
carved for each other; you must mistake
this charity for the rest of your life

until I release you to the fire, sparks
catching, for you cannot escape
the times you live in,

smoke will creep through windows,
infiltrate sheets; you will cough over
convictions, choke on burning hypocrisy,

complement the fire one ideal at a time
until you are baseless, brittle;
you will see those you love dragged,

go wild and embrace the flames
until you are alone inside your frame,
bronzed and scabbed but underneath

you are soft as clay and you can't stop
saying sorry, your shadow crossing
another's as you cross the square

until you notice the play of light between
shadows and pigeons daring for a crumb
and you yourself look up.

Block Party Between COVID Waves

My husband and I break
the spider web on our front door
and step outside.

We, too, must look older, more wrinkled.
The neighbors in the yellow house
have forgotten our names, too,
which breaks the ice somehow.
I find myself laughing.
I find myself smiling at the sound
of others laughing.

One boy, then two more, rush past,
waving Nerf guns. A toddling curly top
coos over the neighborhood tom,
while other children decorate bikes with streamers.

From windows, I've watched these children playing,
followed their tantrums, negotiations, merriment.
I smile at Samantha running toward me
to retrieve a ball, but she looks away
with something like fear.
She sees me as a stranger.
Stranger danger.

After sunset, we adults sit in a circle
slapping mosquitos, tipping beers.
We cannot see expressions only shapes.
Truths slip out.
My mother, brother, best friend.
COVID, heart attack, cancer.

My son, my daughter, myself.
Drugs, anxiety, despair.

We go home exposed,
drunker than we intended.
The spider has returned and is weaving
another web across our door,
which we must break to get back in.

Our house dark and silent
except for a lone cricket trapped in our basement
chirping and waiting,
chirping and waiting.

Stumbling After

The cottonwoods let loose as if by command,
shaking stems, freeing bleached bristles,
hundreds of skirted blossoms,
a feathery snow tumbling west
in a disorganized march.

Fairies, I recall. Lock one in my fist,
whisper a wish, and set her on her way.
I would stumble after until she swung
around a tree, rose against the sun,
and I lost her.

A barbecue at a coworker's,
my friend Paul looks up where cumulus clouds
float like puffs of meringue.

"I'm a chemist, a scientist," he says,
knowing I know but needing to explain.
"Even the color of grass, my hand grasping this cup.
Atoms reacting, ions bonding."

Cancer has shaded his skin ashen, etched out
his flesh so I can see his cheekbones work
as he talks. "Not sure anymore,
even saw a minister," he says, bursting into
what I think is laughter and realize
is gasping, his lungs squeezing
each breath for oxygen.

All I can do is pretend not to notice,
try to focus on the curly-headed nymph,
Paul's daughter, age two, stacking stones near our feet.

She chirps to herself, picks up a stone,
balances it precariously on top another.

A squirrel hurries by and she follows.
Paul rises. They circle a fat oak,
round, round,
the squirrel cackling,
the small girl squealing,
the stooped, thin man in pursuit.

Lot

Old man Lot wanted her to look
back, wanted his wife forever
carved in time, holding the moment
like some prehistoric animal
sculpted in ice.

He tells himself he had no
choice, goes over and over
the scene, her pained shout
a footstep behind, then nothing,
a window slammed shut.

He dreams of her crystallizing
in a shudder of fire,
caught mid-step with her
skirt around her knees,
luminous, incandescent,
a moon figure that gathers light
as evening evaporates.

Months after, he wakes certain
of his love for her,
as when they were nineteen and
the proximity of her hand
made his heart unravel.

Without her around to confuse it,
his love picks up again. Days filtered
through the hushed green of her eyes.
Nights her soft humming
drapes him like a sheet.

Raven

I did not go back to the ark.
Rephrase that: chose not
to go back on the first
day of the 10th month.

I am the symbol few notice,
preferring the erstwhile dove
with the olive branch,
his mesmerizing coo, sleep

inducing chant: waters rocking.
40 days locked with
every creepeth thing that
creepeth the earth.

What is not written:
The birds followed for leagues.
Kingfishers, lesser kestrels,
common cuckoos, bee eaters,

kites, hawks, larks, martins.
A-minor shrieks punctuating the squall,
sodden wings flagging,
talons tearing the ark's shingles.

Inside their fellows lapped the perimeter,
diving and dipping, stirring a riot
among the hooved and pawed;
a cacophony of roars, bellows, cries.

* *

My kind laughed at first: coarse
cackles following me up the plank.

She believed him, she said,
felt a heaviness pressing.
I followed her with the satin feathers,
the old man an afterthought.

Not the last driven by
a well-turned form.

I believe in a headwind's power.
I sing at the sun's warmth.
I trust in the kindness of shade.

I got on the creaking vessel.
Why is that not enough?

To and fro I go until
the waters dry up.
Every preacher requires
a wayward soul.

II

Sonogram

Allowed to speak, my breast lights up
a three-quarter moon startling in its insistence.

I imagine the tête-à-tête, my ear insensitive
to high-pitched pleas.

Hello?
        Hello ...
In there?
        In there ...

The reply bouncing round ducts and lobules
merging whole a black-and-white still.

The awkwardness of running into someone
who once saw right through me,

but I have moved on just moments later
I am no longer myself.

Is that what made us hurry from the cavern?
Remember, we had been laughing at the echo

mocking us mocking the moment,
tossing out slogans only to hear them thrown back:

If I were
              were werrre ...
an Oscar Meyer
              Oss carrcarr Mii yerr yerr
Weiner
              Wein nerr nerr ...

Or was it when the echo separated?

The radiologist in the dark pointing
at the black-and-white image,

a constellation of stars near my nipple,
suspicious likely cancerous pattern.

My cells changing the conversation,
tired of being told what's what.

Home

For my mother

Days after you die, two light bulbs
burn out, one after the other.

I listen to the darkness
envelope the squandered glow.

Weeks later, a ladybug crawls
the frosted window.

I pause to study her spots,
find the warmth of the winter sun.

Mid-March, thunder cracks,
a bygone voice.

I open the door to dankness
under the melting snow,

knowing you'd be here,
each storm part and parcel

of the one we welcomed together
the summer I left home,

rain splashing us through
the porch screens, neither of us

moving inside, knowing we would
set in motion the irretrievable.

How could I not know,
my hand grasping the railing,

blue veins ropy and raised,
I would find your hand.

John Appleseed Speaks His Mind

Some say I'm crazy, an old
sugar sack on my back, toes
sticking out my soles.

Whisper it was malaria, a woman,
a mule kicked me in the head,
changed my thinking on things.

But a bruised apple was what
woke me to the gift
of sweetness shared.

Times the cold camps near,
comes easy to believe doubts
of folks who see different.

My kickin round pal Zach can't
get past the tartness. Sweet Cin
serves apples sliced, thinks it

improper to chaw a chunk. I just
know when I finger the slick seeds
in my pocket I'm right somehow.

I see apple tree linking apple tree,
blooming white in spring,
a lady's nightgown in moonlight.

Blackbirds will jamboree past
dawn, and when the apples burst
red, children will shimmer up

trunks to shake branches,
apples dropping in time
to rolling pins slapping dough.

Uprising

Teeny tiny, unintelligible
from a speck.
Each tri-apple ant
a farsighted blur,
in formation a running,
ceaseless ticker tape
emerging from under
a floor board to
      behind the couch
           around the table
                across the stove
                    up
               down
        the fridge
     into the cat's bowl
and back again.

I vacuum and scour,
wipe out dozens on hundreds
but the parade returns,
silent but rattling.

"You are big with reserves of fat.
You toss bags of untouched food.
You are armed with weapons of destruction."

"We are little, just itty bitty.
We are poor and unarmed.
We are many, many more."

          **

A teardrop of a country
I never bothered to know,
a street vendor sets himself ablaze
because they took his vegetables
because they cast him aside
one too many times.
The smoldering shame of how
he let them define him:

          speck

This is how revolutions begin.
Not with a bang,
but a dismissal.

As I battle the crowds at the mall,
a president is fleeing to Paris.

As I walk my 10,000 steps a day,
copycats douse themselves in gasoline.

As I surf for a distraction,
thousands on thousands gather in a square.

    **

Being five,
being intrigued with all things insect,
my son takes matters into his own hands,
sets traps of raisins under radiators
and waits.

Additional troops arrive.
They crawl under our cuffs,

faint tickles that erupt in
slaps and swearing.
They float in our soup, die in
our undergarments.
They invade the coffee maker,
their minuscule bodies indistinguishable
from the black grounds
we spit in the sink.

My son captures them in Tupperware,
pokes holes in the lids with a fork.

We debate inside and outside:
"Squirrels always outside ... Can you imagine the mess?
Cats and dogs inside and outside.
Mice outside ... OK a caged pet at Johnny's house.
Ants outside, not inside
except OK an ant farm for your birthday."

"But who says?" My son asks.
"I do," I say, and he slinks away.

    **

How many specks before
I pause to name them?
    Terrorists?
        Freedom fighters?
To envision something I never considered,
the dots adding up like a Seurat painting,
all the points of color combining
to form a variegated version
of what's right in front of me.

**

The man at the hardware store explains:
The poison is sweet to the workers
who forage for food,
they won't be able to resist it.

Wingless workers having never had
children of their own
will hurry back to the nest
to share the candy with the queen
and her offspring, and
in their hopes of something more,
they wipe out the colony.

**

An army hazes a square.
It knows no other way.

**

I hesitate before leaving food uncovered.
The ants' absence strange at first.
But within hours, it's as if they were never here.

**

The next spring, a single ant on the counter.
One day later, a trail.

Maud Gonne's Tabby

The cat as a rule avoided poets,
but she put up with Yeats's effusiveness
for her mistress's sake, taking his pets
and coos with a hunter's fine-tuned patience.

She knew an easy mark when she saw one,
and she was in no hurry. The cat loved
watching Maud yank the bard's heart as he spun,
to her keen ear, hamstrung songs of clipped doves.

What did the poet think? That her mistress
could be bound and wound, a muse on demand,
drooling tail-wagger awaiting his kiss.
A bird as free as Maud does not land

but to tease, and with a flitter of tail
has you clawing heights, mewling after gales.

Exponential Decay

"The orange tastes like a refrigerator," my son says,
spitting out his bite and pretending to gag,
and though I have never tasted a refrigerator
I know what he means.

The orange tastes like the plastic it was wrapped in.
And though I have never eaten plastic,
the conjured smell fills my nostrils, dripping down
my throat, a flavor like food stored and forgotten,

seasoned with the sweat of last week's leftovers,
the lamentations of a pepper rotting in the vegetable bin,
unsealed hopes of Tupperware that all
can be contained and preserved.

My overstuffed brain churning with caffeine
links to Miss Havisham's petrified wedding cake.
The jilted bride from Dickens stopping the clocks at 20 to
    nine.
What she might have done with polypropylene.

"I can't eat it," my son says. "I'll never eat another
orange ever, ever." The past enclosing him at age six.
I pull out one of my mother's scrapped sayings:
"Enough with the drama."

I can't give in, or he could lose out: the delight of
oranges, a life spent without the sweet juice dripping
between his fingers, the squirt of citrus in the dead
of winter, the taste like a comeback.

He pushes the slices to the edge of his plate,
a synthetic sheen settling on us. This could go on forever,
molded in polymer, a mother and son encased
with their own microbes for untold half-lives.

Insomnia

I smell her in our bed,
his Insomnia.
He wrestled with her
all night and now sleeps
tangled in twisted sheets.

I get up before the sun
and go about my tasks.
There's pride in knowing
the second to flip a flapjack,
cajole a child.

It will be hours before
he wakes, and he'll look
straight through us
as if we were the mirage,
his wife and children.

Is she with him now?
It's all he talks about,
how he can't get over her,
locks sheer green
like a willow's tentacles
moments before bloom,
her muggy perfume the question
before a downpour.

But I am not innocent.
By evening I am succumbing.
A heaviness traces my thighs
as I lift a load of laundry,
then a salacious dozy swoon

that I allow to sweep me away
before my son jostles me
back to *Charlotte's Web.*

Finally, the lights are off.
My husband and I peck
across the stretch of bed
and I roll over, reaching
for my daemon's grasp,
sweet Sleep.
He never denies me.

A Suburban Winter
Senyru Sequence

first snow
leftover leaves
curl into cups

       her husband debates
       storm windows rattling
       she dons a sweater

staring contest
with a squirrel
broken by agendas

       wind gathers
       speed round the tower—
       a bite in his kiss

snowflake by snowflake
she barely recognizes
herself

       a prayer
       over the plowed parking lot
       teeth chattering

out of the cold
she peels off layers
electric sparks

      across an ice patch
      he reaches for her
      gloved hand

spring mud
faint calligraphy
of bird tracks

Boogie Board

He paddles the boogie board past the drop off
into the face of the wave that rises

to knock out the horizon before it hesitates,
lip snarling, before snatching

its next prey, and you shout his name into
the bellow, sinking in the slipping sand

as the wave crests, barreling down on him:
It will break him against the rocks, it will pull

him to the depths. You've stopped breathing,
every white cap turning up empty.

Out of nowhere he coasts on his belly to you
gangling and glistening, not as small as you recall.

How you dote and dare, both pulling him from
and pushing him back to the break, same as

when he stole his first steps from you,
lunging for dust petals in a sunbeam.

Search Engine Optimization

The new boss believes in traffic.
If we would agree to the keywords
that feed the web spiders, they will lasso
and dangle us like a beacon.
Our winky-dink trade journal, beloved
by a faithful following of hospital CFOs,
will lure the hungry, scattered masses
who do not know they want our advice
on Medicare reimbursement.

My colleagues are editing in their heads.
I recognize the distracted stare of those
transposing a phrase. A few rouse
when the boss quips "total page views."
"They will come," he says. "They just need
to know we are here." I am skeptical
but hold my tongue because everything
is filtered through Vonnegut whom
I'm rereading to recapture a tingling
feeling of comradery from years ago.

"So it goes," Vonnegut says. "Goes it so,"
I reply, and we giggle in the time warp
I've created. Then Vonnegut nods
toward Billy Pilgrim who is walking
Dresden pre-fire in a fur cloak and silver
army boots, and I recoil. I don't want
to be a fool of fate clothed in shiny handouts
as the world flames out. Before I know it,
I am talking out loud: "Why attract visitors
who won't find anything meaningful?"

The new boss looks at me with a blank
expression. I interpret: "What about time
on page?" "Yes," he says, "of course,"
and tosses out "bounce rates" to check
my SEO lingo. My colleagues look nervous.
I have broken the unspoken rule: never
extend a meeting. They just want to leave at five,
seek their own beacons of possibility.

Vonnegut starts a new chapter.
I am sitting at the salon with aluminum foil
woven in my hair. I am getting lowlights,
dark brown streaks to hide my graying mop.
"If it makes you feel good, do it," my husband says,
trying to guess what I want because any answer
he gives, he will lose, for how can he know
the fickle mind of a woman losing her looks to time.

In the lighted mirror, my foiled locks
appear to simmer as if broiled.
My 20-some self arrives to tell my 50-some self
that I'm embarrassing her with silly vanities.
She wanted to be known for her depths and
asks Vonnegut why I'm trying to re-capture the
tingling feeling of a stranger's ogling stare.
"Goes it so," Vonnegut says.

For he knows that time, the blessed mother
of all dualities, works like a teeter-totter,
the present being the fulcrum that sees and
saws. Sometimes you get trapped mid-air
by the weight of what was or should be,
dangling a lame duck, the only choices

to slide slowly toward the other side
or jump and let the other bang her bum.

My 70-some self gets this. She looks in the
mirror and recommends lipstick. "It pulls
the eye from the wrinkles." But 20-some wants
to be loved for my crow's feet, for my wisdom.
"I'll give you wisdom," says 70-some.
"You were most meaningful when you parted
the crowd in that dress strung of only keywords."
My 20-some smiles demurely.
"That was sexy. But I felt so small after."

All the seesawing and chemicals cause me
to lose my equilibrium. The mirror opens
a playground. There's my boss trying to rhyme
swings with Billy. My office mates politely
taking turns down the slide.

Vonnegut pushes away the children
on the merry go round, his irascible brows
good-natured frowns. He points to a freckled girl
on the monkey bars, and I recognize my 7-some self,
swinging upside down, spinning alluring tales
of this meaningful life I expect for myself.

Blood Draw

Someone is hammering overhead
with admirable precision:

bang one onethousand bang,

waking the pulse near my throat.
But my heart refuses to keep tempo:
one bang behind or one bang ahead.

The blood draw room is painted grey,
encouraging the only decoration,
an oversized photo to step forward.

The end of a pier merging into an
expanse of silvery blue. Not a
single ripple disturbs the calm.

I have been on that pier or one like it,
a question mark
peering into the murk.

What is a pier but our attempt to walk
on water, to keep something solid
between us and the drop off?

The needle pricks and blood fills
the tube. A small wave crests
before more blood rushes in.

I've always preferred the surf.
My feet gripping the sand only
to be knocked down, run ashore.

It's become a habit:
this getting up again,
this ruse of another chance

though the results are clear:
The banging will go on long after
the pier gives way beneath me.

The Sisters Part Ways

Flapping bulbous glands,
fat-encased breasts with
your nipple-areola complex.
Since you sprouted, you've
insisted on going first,
two bulls-eyes dominating
the conversation.

Water-retaining tetons,
stretch-marked mammillas with
your sure-bet erogenous zones.
You came too soon, and I tried
to hide. My mother's finger
down my spine, shocking me
from an adolescent slump.

Satin-swaddled cleavage,
pillow-soft cantaloupes with
your handy headrest.
You bulged with pride from
your demi cups when he bent
toward me, taught me the power
in skin tight.

Stiff-saluting chill detectors,
sweater-stretching air bags with
your unused spare parts.
You blamed me. Our son latching
the bottle's latex teat. His green eyes
locking mine, unaware
yet what I can never be.

Wire-supported ying-yangs,
starting-to-sag Berthas with
your mercurial monthly swings.
The right a rebel in middle age,
risking it all, flirting with cancer
to own a tale separate from
her sanctimonious sister's.

Simple

The priest called us "simple" at our wedding.
He kept coming back to that word
in his homily on love and marriage.
I took it as an insult, a dismissal.

"Look at the nice, harmless couple
entering their inconsequential life together,"
I ranted on our honeymoon, a perspiring beer
dripping down my arm in the dive
we'd stumbled on in Old San Juan.

"What does he know of us, of love?" I asked,
and that night we upturned the sheets
to prove our beyond ordinary passion.

That was when I saw couples separated
by restaurant tables, silently stabbing
individual salads and panicked, mistaking
the foreshadower's nod for a warning.

I would grab your hand and launch
debates on the day's headlines
or half-remembered history lessons,
anything but nothing to say to each other.

I did not know you would become
my relief from words. For sentences
trail into paragraphs, chapters flutter
forth, heaping page after page.
Half our marriage, we've stood stunned,
pebbles at the beck and call of currents.

In the interim, the hour or two a day
when nothing is demanded, we sit silent,
and I catch you glancing at me
as I turn to glance at you.

What can I say? I was an idiot.
It's taken me 20 years to accept
the priest's prognosis:
Love simplifies.

Parenting Styles

Season after season, flowers seed.
Petals spent, stalks shiver
in the anticipated breeze, shaking their offspring
from their heads.

They have given them all they can.
What's the point of worrying?
This is what angiosperms do.

Besides the seeds are dormant through the worst of it:
The dispersion.
The scarification by shifting soil and ice.
The long thirst and swelling imbibition.

They have enough food packed in their cotyledons
to get them started, assuming they do not
dig themselves in too deeply
or become snacks for the birds,
their meristems will pull them up from the darkness
at the first hint of warmth.

Humans are more like turf grasses,
fibrous roots twined tight.
It takes a sharp spade to slice us from our young.

Writing for the Man

When my voice becomes co-opted.
After they tell me what to pen
and where to forfeit.

When I come home and everyone
wants the last little bit of me,
I take the remains of the day

to the alley. I heave our bulging
bag of composting fragrances
as I would an offering,

flies gathered greedily
about the mouth of the steel bin
that emphatically snaps

our uneaten leftovers, chip bags
emptied on sly, stockings with a run in
the thigh, swept-up crumbs and spills.

This middle-class conjecture,
fata morgana: our garbage
disappears every Thursday

as if it never happened.
Out here, fences on either side,
I have only so many choices.

South past a tom eyeing sparrows
splashing. North where the sullen
goth kid tinkers with an engine.

Or up — westward over cascading
recyclables, baseball floating in a
window, screech of a newborn learning

to sleep — to the sycamores,
seven in a row rising above it all,
their bark stripped from them as they grew,

and all they have to present
to the setting sun is bone, bleached
calcified branches beginning to leaf.

It's a divestiture of artifice,
chicanery, avarice, blood thirst
for a return.

It's a prayer for a breath
rinsed of the bottom line, distilled
of my hems and haws, knuckles

scraped by constant compromise.
The tom is making his move.
The babe is quiet.

Back east across our untilled garden,
the kitchen light turns on.
A buoyancy unbolts my throat.

Every day should shed
its pretense like the sycamores
naked and reaching.

III

Kisses
> *For Craig*

That song again,
and I am in that kiss
again that felt so right
but for the right person.

The sudden downpour,
dash from the bar
down the lamp-lit street,
breathless and laughing
at our sodden clothes,
smell of mud hungry
beneath melting snow,
and what the hell
shock of his lips
quieting my shivers.

A kiss that might
have been scripted,
a kiss that still wakes
the hair on my thighs,
a kiss I do not regret
but for you, the right person,
loading the dishwasher while
I part from a young man's
arms whose name
I struggle to remember.

The piano man builds
his case, coaxing strings
and horns, a baritone's confession
from some damp corner

into a crescendo of yearning,
like the blackbirds this morning,
dozens of them rising
off electrical wires
to ride gusts of a storm,
forks of lightening
dramatizing the choreography,
and me grounded
in our four-door sedan.

We have our kisses, of course,
the memories we recount
beneath the goose down.
Remember, that first kiss
in your old Dodge Dart
sunk in the bucket seats,
or that record hot day
when we couldn't stop
kissing on the wall to wall.

The luck of you
humbles me, leaves
me reaching for your hand
in the TV's haze,
beneath the kitchen table.
This should be enough.
But then a melody, a scent,
the sight of our son's
gangly limbs cuts
to the swiftness.

Kiss me,
like we are strangers
beneath shorn trees unable

to slow the belting rain.
Kiss me, like my name
is easily forgotten but not
the slope of my hip
you trace then yank tight.
Kiss me, before
the song ends, and we
remember ourselves.

Spotting Hobos

Look between, on top of boxcars,
unshaven men in patched, torn
clothes, ready to jump on the
slightest whim, an unusually green
patch of grass, a red-headed
woman, the smell of a steak frying.

Down on their luck, my dad says,
and we understand luck is budgeted,
parceled out, something that must
be courted, enticed. The commission
that sends him peddling contraptions,
brings him home whistling bebop or
staring at some far-off point.

It becomes a game. Stopped on the way
to pick up groceries, drop dry cleaning,
post bills, a freight train plows past,
wheels screeching, horns blasting,
a seismic tremor that cuts our town in half,
pharmacy, shoe store blotted out.

My sisters and I take turns spotting the
travelers, "There on top of the red car,"
or "There inside the yellow one,"
shouting over squeals of metal,
the gate's unceasing howl. The trees,
our Chevy, even our bones vibrating.

With a running start, we could catch that
empty cattle car, land in the scratchy hay,

wheels beneath us beating four time,
buildings and strip malls clicking by.

End up chasing waves near Monterey,
the breeze heavy with the sea, salty, palatable.
Or camped in the Tetons, slim Aspens
fanning leaves, silver, green,
a layer of stars blinking.

The Other Side

for Alex

You and I pick one by one
the wet stones glittering the shore,
greedily pocketing the shine,
until our shorts bulge
like hamster cheeks,
and we walk bow-legged
to the car, turning every few feet
to look back at the lake,

as if her shifting moods could
not be summoned at will, as if
for days we won't be brushing
sand from our every crevice.
But you pause again to look
before we breach, and I stop
to memorize you, my son,
before you grow again.

We are flatlanders, dwellers of
paved prairies. We do not take
large churning bodies of water
or even hills for granted. And this
is our Great Lake, our absolute location
between Polaris and Crux, always
to the east of us except this one
week a year when it sits west,

the shift in longitude fluid as a lane
change, and we see the expressway
has thinned to two streams, and can

you believe the lake is behind those
pines? What if we forgot towels.
We can buy more. Poor kitty
left behind, but we will be okay
with the lake by our side.

The car is overstuffed with a whiff
of adolescent boy and something
sticky is underfoot. The mattresses
will be lumpy, booze will pour
copiously, and there will be rancorous
meltdowns and direct kicks
under the table and a chance of rain
that dredges boredom.

This is why we collect the stones
you tell me as I once told you, bending
to select a perfect circle, a burnished
hole on your palm. A reminder.
In late summer, at a certain time of day,
the sun plays off the washed-up stones
and they shine one by one as one,

and it's as if we never left. The lake having
a way of not being there and then being
there fully without excuses. She greets us,
loaded down with folding chairs, pails
and shovels, boogie boards. A bustling
matriarch enfolding us in her remembered
embrace without a pause to her chatter.

The lake is wild today, waves dragging
us down. The lake is calm today, us
the only ripples. The lake is somewhere

in between. And we play our roles
perfectly. Your father's squeal wading in,
your brother atop a crest, you and
your cousins digging and splashing
and coaxing us to the sand bar.

At some point, the sun angles to catch
the blond hairs on your burnt
shoulders. You are laughing, and one
by one we start to laugh as one.
That is what we remember when,
back home, we un-pocket the stones,
faded and rough to touch.
This capacity we have to glow.

How to Die Like a Collapsing Star

For my father

You teach us the art of long good-byes,
distract us with what's inescapable.
Even when you have vanished from our eyes
we will feel your gravitational pull,

find ourselves humming jazz tunes you whistled,
our new-found aches groaning with your go-to
counsel: "Never get old." How we chuckled.
But who's laughing now as we pay what's due.

Everyone born of stars returns to stars:
As you collapse, we feel ourselves torn
from the remaining light to something barred,
concealed behind the event horizon.

You must hang on till the wait is over,
and you pull to you every last one you love.

My Big Idea

I had it all figured out when I was nine.
Between writing storybooks with
gold-plated covers, I would have
eight children who wanted to play
my games, not like my sisters who wanted
to play their games, and last but not least,
I was going to start a village on
the grassy green we circled
whenever we exited the highway home.

All that empty space and no one there,
only dandelions or cattails,
depending on the month.
They would come from all over.
The poor, the sick, the sad.
It wouldn't matter if they spoke languages
I couldn't understand. I would cook
pots of spaghetti and smile kindly
as I filled their plates.

But I didn't know what to do about
the lepers, the ones Jesus healed,
the ones I needed to welcome, embrace,
if my village was going to be filled with love
like I felt before the sun moved
from our left to our right,
my father rotating the wheel,
my mother turning to check on us
in the back seat,

and my plan would unravel
before the end of the exit

every time I got to the lepers
reaching out hands missing digits,
faces covered in scales.
I would imagine the smell,
all those people, a stench of someone else's
sweat multiplied by thousands,
and the plates that kept coming back
for more and more and
more of me.

That's when I would turn and swat
whichever sister happened to be next
to me, call her a stupid idiot
because she was unfortunate
to be sitting between
the person I wanted to be
and the person I kept realizing I was
no matter how many times we exited
round the grassy green,
the same untouchable answer.

Cardinal

The cat gets its bird because
I hang the feeder again
after the storm dumps snow enough
to muffle all sound but a weak
chirp, and I spot the crouched red
beat in our white-cloaked tree.

He looks utterly alone,
feathers fluffed against gusts
that reanimate fallen snow,
whirling skirmishes collapsing
short of a dance, and I wonder
after the cardinal's mate, a gentler
shade of red.

Weeks ago, she and he were flitting
about our yard. That was before
I put the feeder away because
the orange tabby kept coming
around, and I found myself outside
in robe and slippers banging
a steel pot and I felt a fool

after the flurry of wings subsided,
after the fur ball skittered
under the fence, and my own cat,
Annabelle, met me at the door.
I swear she looked embarrassed.

"I was trying to save the birds," I said.
Annie gave me a cynical stare and
walked away. It takes a stray to know

who saves whom. I open her cans but
she does most of the work in our family.

So I took the feeder down to prove
my cat wrong, that I could live without
the birds if it meant saving them.

Each morning, the greedy chirping
dimmed a little more. The dark-eyed junco
stopped coming round, followed by
the woodpeckers and chickadees.

Then on cue, sparrows stopped pecking
at remnants of seed in the slush
and rose in a whoosh and were gone,
leaving my backyard empty,
a colorless, frigid stillness.

The shivering cardinal was the excuse
I needed to put the feeder back up.
Isn't that how the world works?
I help you. You help me.

Already, moments after I see the chubby
tabby plunge for the bird,
I'm thinking how I might keep the feeder hung,
continue luring my cheerful guests,
surely I feed more than are killed,
surely I am allowed this one small joy,
opening the shade to signs of life,

as I trudge shovel in hand for a burial,
the still red beat staining the snow.

Bumper Crop

Only fools seek signs
in the elapsing days of August,

crickets on rewind,
humidity's woolen drag,

squirrels draped as if
dead over branches

in the unmoving canopy.
I squat between garden rows,

a supplicant from the frosty
hollows of central air.

It's been weeks since I've been
outside other than passing

door to car, car to door.
There's a kind of poverty in

diligence. The way one check mark
seizes another. Between scrounging,

the hazy light shifts, and it's time
to harvest what I missed ripening.

Tomatoes overrun their cages,
hairy stalks swabbing my arms.

Into my mouth, I toss
a cherry, and the ball

splits its skin, exploding seeds
and flesh against my teeth.

There is something more
than sweetness here.

In the aftertaste,
a tartness that bristles.

Only fools seek answers from
wasps buzzing split squash,

hawks circling a striated sky
that stares back mute

at me kneeling bereft despite
the bounty stretching my shirttails.

I don't realize I'm crying until the salt
reaches my lips and something loosens

in me I didn't know I was holding
back. You again.

If I say I believe
will you help me believe?

I used to ride thermals of hymns,
fashion papier-mâché miracles.

I miss that freckled girl. But her God
would bore me short of an hour.

Is that why you only give me
half answers?

A knot of sparrows tugs me up
only to unravel.

I carry inside my pickings,
the screen door latching.

For hours, the scent of stalks,
pungent, acrid, honest

infuses my clothes,
clings to my skin

until I strip and shower off
the reminder I need saving.

Tarzan Goes to His Resting Grounds

> Johnny Weissmuller,
> Olympic swimmer,
> famous for his portrayal
> of Tarzan in the movies,
> died today ...
> —*Chicago Sun Times*

The leopard skin is pressed and cleaned
protected by a plastic pack,
stored with the medals and clippings,
safe from moths and damp.

He waits, watches waves sliding toward
his lawn chair, sips tonic to keep cool.
Twelve-year-old girls are breaking
his records by the length of a pool.

An ice cream truck singing soprano lulls
him asleep, a polka-dotted girl
chasing waves screams laughter
and he is in the jungle,

flying behind the chimps among the trees.
Soon he will see the hallowed land
where elephants go to die;
plaster tusks set in sand.

Child's Body Found in Park Lagoon, Chicago

Pick the blue cornflowers,
swish and sway of wild primrose.
Pick what is sweet and helps you forget.

I'll sit with you, as long as it takes.
Sing you songs of crimson clover
and ox-eyed daisies until you hear
the dead calling, the other little ones
playing hide and seek in the cattails.
I helped them cross as I'll help you.

You know me. I whispered in your ear
whenever the scary man yelled.

Let me comb out the muck, braid
a crown of dandelions for your curls,
sew you a dress of golden yarrow.
Your story is just beginning.

I'll rub balms of marigold and chamomile
on your bruises, tell you tales of
sweet William and his black-eyed Susan
so you'll stop thinking about
the steel weight that dragged
you under the water lilies
into the silent fury of tadpoles.

Pick hummingbirds kissing the poppies,
white moths drinking their full.
Pick my hand.

Unfettered

"What a life," my husband says
about the horses grazing downhill,
dew deflecting sunlight.

We tread sideways down the slope,
weary of mole burrows snaking,
to get some of what they've got
out here in the pasture, a taste
of leisure that will be ours,
not so long until we are unfettered.

When we get closer, I see the mist
that glows round the horses
mingles and shifts with flies.
A jolt of dung smacks me,
fresh piles exhaling.

I hold out an apple,
and a hard-worn mare walks
to the barb-wire fence,
her thick lips dry and soft
as worn wood, a flicker
of tooth against my palm.

When she raises her head
speckled with silver, I see flies
drinking the sweat between her eyes,
no bucolic wistfulness in her gaze
only the distracted thoughts of one
whose work is not yet done.

Shadows

Last light, and us intercepting the light
as we walked. Mother and son.

I remember stamping on your shadow,
and your delight as your small silhouette

got out from under me, stretching
to a giant's fierce semblance.

We wove shadows all the way home.
But now we're always out of step.

"It's coming down hard," I offer,
pulling off my boots.

Your earbuds block my existence.
"So lovely, the snow," I say, louder.

The me I cannot help but be
lingering like yesterday's onions.

You roll your eyes. Your boy face
subsumed by the man you are becoming.

Only last year you pummeled
me with snowballs,

and I chased you giggling
back to our fort.

I am trying not to press, I am trying
to keep my demands brief: "Shovel. Please."

I am learning to let you slam the door,
wade through snow solo.

You will spew and froth and stumble,
your breath freezing your nose hairs.

This is the tipping point.

The stars won't blink. You must.
I am learning to be a memory that prompts

you to look for your shadow thin and tall,
a passing chance to catch yourself.

I am the plea in the wind's callous whistling.

Let your shadow rise as for an embrace
before evening swipes your image.

You and I

Soon mostly sky,
the last gold
gripped against gusts.

A shock how
much the canopies
held us in,

the towering oaks
disoriented,
shorn stalks flailing.

Friday and the
doors open,
the push and pull

to get out from under,
to break into a gallop
a soprano, a curse,

the only certainty
that I am missing out,
that someone is telling

a tale and others are
starting to laugh,
that someone else

is walking up to
the flannelled shoulders
in the crowd.

I have known them all.
The sun-stamped necks
stretching from collars,

trepid tenors
coaxing deeper at
my fluttering titter,

brusque hands,
thick fingers
guiding my elbow.

The wait for the call.
I have counted our days
in silence between rings.

Since when did you
become the overseer
of the lines?

You rake the leaves
into piles for bagging,
calculate calories

before pouring a wine.
The blue a perfect pitch
above the maple's

thinning blades.
Only you are surprised
to still find me here

as a cloud bank moves in
healing the
sky a scab.

Looking Up from the News

She expects smoke creeping toward her through the shorn trees.

She wouldn't be surprised to feel the floor tremble,

to open the door and find scraps floating along the biting gust —

palm-size remnants, a congregation of charred color.

She listens for a retreat of engines gaining elevation, and the screams,

the screams melding into stadium rumble.

Yet children are walking to school. A boy steals

his friend's cap and runs away. The neighbor exits

his door at 8:02 a.m. as usual and folds into his car.

A flock of sparrows play harmony

to forsythia that must have bloomed overnight. Another

Monday with its pent-up trepidations,

lamentations for the lost weekend, its stored chance for an hour,

a moment to catch the eye of another,

to delve into the sheen starting to spread toward her.

An ordinary day she would have passed by

but for this debt. This lease she can only repay by grabbing what was taken from another without recourse.

Acknowledgments

Below is a list of poems in this book that have been previously published or have won awards.

"Bumper Crop" was published by Pine Row Press — Poetry Issue #5, Summer 2022.

"Child's Body Found in Park Lagoon" was published in *Encore: Prize Poems of the NFSPS 2020*.

"Crazy" was published in *Naugatuck River Review*, Summer 2013.

"Exponential Decay" was published in *The Penman Review*, December 2022.

"Hysteranthous" was published in *Bethlehem Writers Roundtable*, Spring 2022.

"Kisses" was published in *The Penman Review*, January 2023.

"Looking Up from the News" was published in *Subprimal*, Spring 2016.

"Lot" was published in *Pittsburgh Quarterly Online*, 2003. This journal is no longer in existence.

"The Other Side" was published in *The Penman Review*, January 2023.

"Raven" was published in *Spoon River Poetry Review*, Winter 2021 (46.2) issue.

"Religion Arrives in the Subdivision" was published in *Meat for Tea*, March 2016.

"A Sculptor to the Sculpted" was published by *The Woodward Review*, Spring 2023.

"September Clouds" was published in *The Sunlight Press* on April 7, 2022.

"Sonogram" was published in *Neat*, Spring 2014.

"Spotting Hobos" was published in *Pittsburgh Quarterly Online*, 2003. This journal is no longer in existence.

"Tarzan Goes to His Resting Grounds" was published in *Neat*, Spring 2014.

"The Unraveling Script" was published in *Atticus Review* on March 31, 2021, under the title "The Unraveling of Cursive."

"Uprising" was published in *Epiphany*, Spring 2017, and in *Meat for Tea*, March 2016.

"Writing for the Man" was published in *Hamilton Stone Review*, Fall 2022.

"You and I" was published in *Meat for Tea*, March 2016.

About the Poet

Maggie Kennedy spends early mornings staring out a window at a row of 100-year-old sycamore trees. Sometimes a poem comes along. Her work has appeared in numerous publications, including *Epiphany, Spoon River Poetry Review,* and *Atticus Review*. She honed her craft at Eastern Illinois University and the University of Chicago, earning degrees in English and creative writing. This is her first book of poems. She lives in the Chicago suburbs with her family and works as a professional writer and editor.

Cover: Photo and design by Alex Van Dyke

Made in the USA
Monee, IL
18 May 2024